Reflections in the Son

Reflections in the SON

Mary Irwin

BROADMAN PRESS
Nashville, Tennessee

© Copyright 1985●Broadman Press
All rights reserved
4257-10
ISBN: 0–8054–5710–0
Dewey Decimal Classification: 242
Subject Heading: MEDITATIONS
Library of Congress Catalog Card Number: 85-4109
Printed in the United States of America

Library of Congress Cataloging in Publication Data

Irwin, Mary, 1938-
  Reflections in the Son.

  1. Meditations.   I. Title.
BV4832.2.I79   1985   242   85-4109
ISBN 0-8054-5710-0

With love to the
5 Js
for giving me most of the material for this book:
Joy, Jill, Jim, Jan, and **Joe**

Foreword

Mary Irwin is a woman who knows how to pray earnestly for the big problems in her life—safety for her husband as he sped down the first lunar highway, restoration for a daughter who was running down sin's freeway, and the direction for herself as her marriage began to ride the road to divorce. These were the desperate prayers of a woman whose world was once in pieces as she described them in her first book, *The Moon Is Not Enough.*

Now we meet Mary Irwin (with her world back together), the author who sees God in the small, ordinary details of her life—birds, snowstorms, food, gardens, houseplants, seashells, pedestrians, hikes, butterflies, baby chicks, and other common daily occurrences—as well as extraordinary events. Mary relates her daily living to her continual walk with the Lord.

Someone has commented, "I can cope with the crises; it's the daily hassles that overwhelm me." *Reflections in the Son* will enable you to see Mary's deep spiritual commitment to please God in the routine of business, the daily grind of family responsibilities, and the maze of human relationships. If you're not in the habit of seeking and seeing God in the trivial detail of everyday living, then maybe He's waiting for you to find Him in these pages of *Reflections in the Son.*

JACK WYRTZEN
Word of Life

Contents

1. It Missed the Shelter   11
2. A Reflection of Your Son   13
3. Was It an Angel?   16
4. Crying Out for Nourishment   18
5. Caught in a Cross Tide   20
6. The Burned Kidney Beans   23
7. No More Strength to Fight   25
8. Grasshoppers and the Tithe   28
9. Dying to Live   30
10. The Good Shepherd   32
11. Lessons from African Violets   34
12. Lessons from Seashells   36
13. Nagging and the Jay   39
14. Truths from Shiny Strawberries   41
15. The Peerless Leader   43
16. Not Seeing but Believing   46
17. Climbing Higher   48
18. Divine Molding   50
19. Rebirth   53
20. Don't Squeeze!   55
21. The Shepherd's Voice   57
22. Missy Came Back   59
23. Approaching with Confidence   62
24. Flood My Riverbed   64

25. Brokenness and Blessing   67
26. Burden Bearers   70
27. Playing Without Power   72
28. The Fizzled-out Experiment   74
29. Make a Sign!   77
30. Jesus Removes the Stingers   79
31. Angel in the Chasm   81
32. Free as a Bird   83
33. Jesus, the Master Painter   85
34. Near-death on Ararat   89
35. The Severed Branch   92
36. Fortification Against Coyotes   94

1
It Missed the Shelter

The rugged, rocky coastline on the Monterey peninsula can sometimes produce awesome storms, with waves crashing and splashing twenty to thirty feet high. This particular day in January brought one of those rainy storms. Jim and I walked close to the edge of the craggy cliff to photograph the roaring waves. When the roll of film was finished, we walked hand in hand toward our motel room.

Looking over the side of a steep area, we were surprised to see a small bird had landed in the pounding surf. Whatever was it doing there all alone in such a dangerous place? We stood motionless—watching, waiting. A wave would wash it with a fierceness upon the rocks. The bird would shake its little head, fluff its feathers, and struggle to escape the water—but to no avail. It was straining so hard to survive.

I said to Jim, "If we don't help that little fellow immediately, he won't last another three minutes." In the next moments, we decided to try a rescue. Our timing would have to be precise in order to jump ten feet and grab the little bird before the next wave broke. A moment before one of us jumped, another huge wave caught the little one off guard. It pitifully strove but was too weak to fight back. The wave receded and left only white foam. I tried to choke back the tears, even though I had just learned a profound lesson from life. As we continued our walk back to the room, I saw something we had missed on our way out. There were the rest of the birds in a little, protected cove, away from the fierceness of the storm. Why had that young one missed the mark? Didn't he have enough instruction on flying and landing in a storm?

Did he have an adventuresome spirit? I don't know the answer, but I do know that Jesus is my shelter in a time of storm. David had that confidence too, and wrote in Psalms 107:28-31:

> Then they cry unto the Lord in their trouble, and he bringeth them out of their distresses. He maketh the storm a calm, so that the waves thereof are still. Then are they glad because they be quiet; so he bringeth them unto their desired haven. Oh that men would praise the Lord for his goodness, and for his wonderful works to the children of men!

Jesus truly is our only shelter, our protected cove amid fierce storms.

2
A Reflection of Your Son

December 23 the snow began falling softly, silently—
slowly at first, then faster. By evening several inches had
fallen. Our family set out for an after-dinner walk, enjoy-
ing the snowflakes playing on our faces and sticking to
our eyelashes. We strolled along the road and through the
woods near our home, reveling in the fellowship. When
we returned, the children played outside in the snow
while I swept off our walkway.

As I was standing in the echoing darkness, my attention was drawn to the single source of light which fell
across the yard, the large outdoor lamppost on our driveway. Its steady glow was reassuring and inviting, making
a safe place for our children to play and acting as a beacon
against the inky night.

I knew there were many cold, tired, hungry, and lost
people in the world. What would it take for them to see
"a beacon in the dark night"?

I thought how Jesus said:

Ye are the light of the world. A city that is set on an hill
cannot be hid. Neither do men light a candle, and put it
under a bushel, but on a candlestick; and it giveth light
unto all that are in the house. Let your light so shine

before men, that they may see your good works, and glorify your Father which is in heaven (Matt. 5:14-16).

That night I prayed, "Father, help me to be a light that shines as brightly to those who don't know You as our outdoor light that shines for all to see the pathway to our home. Make me glow with the love of Jesus so I may reassure those who are afraid, and help me to act as a beacon against the darkness of this world. Let me always be a reflection of your Son to illuminate the way to Calvary, and thank You for being the 'Light' unto my pathway."

Let us all be *Reflections in the Son.*

3
Was It an Angel?

The ringing of our doorbell pierced the silence of the night. I quickly became conscious enough to jump out of bed, grab my robe, and look at the clock as I ran toward the hallway and the front door. Jim was right behind me. I could see a red police light oscillating through the window, but I couldn't figure out what was going on at 3:00 AM. I knew our children were all in bed fast asleep.

As Jim opened the door a policeman was standing there. "You have a hefty grass fire burning outside," he spoke hastily. "It's already burned two acres. Get your family out; the wind's blowing in the direction of your house. I've already called the fire department." He was gone.

I went downstairs and awakened the children quietly so I wouldn't scare them. Jim went outside as the fire engines arrived. Our county fire department called in two more trucks for assistance. By 5:00 AM the fires were out, and we all fell back into bed, physically and emotionally exhausted.

Around 10 that morning I decided to call the police department and express grateful thanks from our family to the policeman who had been on duty. I was put on hold while an officer checked out who was in our area patrolling so early in the morning. After several minutes he came back on the line and reported, "Lady, there was no one patrolling out in your area last night." I objected, "Yes, there was; he saved our home and our lives." Surely someone had reported the fire to police headquarters. The officer again left the phone to check out the county sheriff's department, returning to the phone with the same story: "Lady, there was no one patrolling your area last night, and no fire was reported." I thanked him and hung up.

I stood there by the phone letting all the information sink into my brain and my heart. Tears filled my eyes as I realized who had been patrolling our area that early morning. The angel of the Lord comes in patrol cars too. "For the Angel of the Lord guards and rescues all who reverence Him" (Ps. 34:7, TLB).

4
Crying Out for Nourishment

When our eldest daughter, Joy, was in the seventh grade, she developed an interesting science project. After choosing four mice, she placed one male and one female in one cage and the other couple in another cage. One pair she fed a poor diet with loads of junk food; the other pair was fed a highly nutritious, balanced diet. Her job was to observe the difference, if any, in their behavior patterns.

As was expected, the two poorly fed mice were extremely nervous and fighting constantly. Their fur was mottled looking, without luster. They could never seem to rest but would tear wildly around their cage, stop and drink copious amounts of water, then fall into an exhausted sleep. When they reproduced, their. offspring were deformed, and the parents ate their babies.

The two well-fed mice showed none of those stressful signs. They didn't fight, bite, and act nasty with each another. They both had shining fur. They didn't tear around in their cage but were found sleeping most of the time. Neither did they drink large amounts of water. When they had offspring, they seemed to be perfect, and the father didn't need to be removed for fear that he would eat his babies.

Watching those mice behaving so erratically made me think of the different kinds of people in this world. What makes some people behave peacefully and others violently? If we compare ourselves to the mice, perhaps "the restless ones" lack proper ingredients in their lives, something they need desperately, something as basic to their survival as the food they eat.

This "something" is none other than Jesus Christ. Just as those frustrated mice were reacting to a need for nourishment, tormented, lonely people are crying out for love and for the nourishment of the Word of God.

We Christians need to feed or disciple those hungry souls God brings into our lives. What a joy to watch a change in their behavior as they decide they too want to live for Jesus. The sparkle highlights their eyes, and their bodies become temples of the Holy Spirit as they understand 1 Corinthians: 6:19-20

Do you not know that your body is a temple of the Holy Spirit, who is in you, whom you have received from God? You are not your own; you were bought at a price. Therefore honor God with your body (NIV).

5
Caught in a Cross Tide

Staniel Cay is a small island approximately sixty miles south of the Grand Bahamas. It can be reached only by boat or private plane.

The water is so clear azure and beautiful that it enticed Jim and me to return a second time for a week of rest.

There are no telephones, television sets, or radios in the four small rental cottages. Anyone staying on the island is almost forced to relax in the sun and water and enjoy the company of others.

We both like collecting seashells, so I encouraged Jim to take me out in a boat to a tiny island during high tide. I had visions of many shells awaiting me. I should have known better—one should never shell hunt during high tide!

Our ten-foot boat, with an unpredictable engine, chugged from Staniel toward the uninhabited island nearly four miles away. Upon arriving we could see that we would have a difficult time bringing in the boat because we were caught in a cross tide. The natives have a special name for that kind of tide since it is most dangerous.

I jumped into the water and pulled the ropes as Jim pushed from behind. The first wave knocked me flat on my back. I scrambled to my feet, but the next wave had begun to fill the boat. It was easy to see that within minutes everything in the boat would float away, and the boat would sink. I kept pulling the ropes, and Jim kept pushing. Each wave broke into the boat. The sand could never hold the anchor; neither could the rocks close by.

Fear gripped me like never before. I cried out to God, "Don't You care that we are going to drown?" I was convinced that if we continued this course of action one or both of us would drown.

The waterlogged boat was almost impossible to pull. The slipping rope was yanking the skin off my hands. I continued to cry out loud to God. Immediately flashing before me were scenes of Jesus and His disciples on the Sea of Galilee during a raging storm. I felt as scared as the disciples had been. Fear drains one's emotional and physical energy quickly. Could I hold on until we had the little boat anchored? "Jesus save us" was all I could say.

On the beach were many small palm trees. I spotted one near me no taller than four feet with the diameter of about three inches: "Little tree, could you possibly hold the anchor rope?" We were trusting the Lord to save us, not the little tree, and immediately Jeremiah 17:7-8 came to my mind:

> Blessed is the man that trusteth in the Lord, and whose hope the Lord is. For he shall be as a tree planted by the waters, and that spreadeth out her roots by the river, and shall not see when heat cometh, but her leaf shall be green; and shall not be careful in the year of drought, neither shall cease from yielding fruit.

With each push of the wave's action and Jim's pushing from behind, we inched the rope closer to the small palm. I wrapped the rope around once, twice, then three times. The boat was secure.

In total exhaustion, we both sat down to rest. We had saved everything in the boat.

In a few moments, Jim was ready to bail out the water and try the engine. We replaced all our picnic items and trusted the Lord to start the engine. It started the first try. Needless to say we didn't get any shells. As we headed toward home, I knew we had been given a far greater gift—the gift of life and God's promises driven straight to our hearts.

6
The Burned Kidney Beans

No one likes burned kidney beans, and I am no exception. I, Mary Irwin, am notoriously known in our family as the "bean burner." For that very reason, my guilty conscience didn't let me prepare them too often. It wasn't that I deliberately let them burn, but I always forgot to keep adding water as they cooked and this day was no exception.

The wind was blowing and howling outside the house while the snow was fast piling into drifts. Jim was out of town, so the children and I snuggled in the master bed while I read a fascinating book to them about modern-day miracles.

I had put on a pot of beans to cook around 10:00 AM, and it was nearly noon. We had become so absorbed in the book I forgot once again to put more water into the beans. Suddenly, I smelled that all-too-familiar burned smell. I had done it again!

I jumped out of bed, hoping to salvage the beans. One stir around the pot told me it was too late. It made me sick with guilt to look at the mess. There were people starving all over the world, and I was about to throw out dinner.

Lord, I thought, *here I have been reading about miracles to the children, do I have enough faith to believe You can do something with this terrible mess I have created?* I knew Jesus' first miracle was at the wedding feast where the supply of wine ran out and He turned water into wine. Here was a perfect opportunity to let the children experience the power of God and a testing of our faith. I called them all into the kitchen, and we gathered around the burned beans while I prayed. "Lord Jesus, I know You turned water into wine, and You still do miracles today. I am asking You to please touch and heal this pot of beans. Please take out the burned taste, so we can eat them for dinner and I won't have to throw them away. Thank You for hearing our prayer and for already answering in Jesus' name, Amen."

I added about one gallon of water to the pot, put it back on the stove to simmer while we all climbed back into bed to finish reading our book. Around 5 PM it was time to check on the beans. I gave them a stir, and the black burn from the bottom was floating all through the beans; they still smelled terrible. My faith was beginning to waver. Praying silently, I reconfirmed my faith and trusted that God had granted our request, even though it didn't look or smell like it. The children were anxiously standing near to see what the outcome would be when I put the first spoonful into my mouth. By faith I believe God healed those beans the moment I put the spoon to my lips and not before.

We all had a generous portion for dinner. Even though the burned black stuff was still floating around the pot, there was not one trace of burn in the flavor.

The psalmist sang, "The Lord will perfect that which concerneth me: thy mercy, O Lord, endureth forever" (Ps. 138:8).

Surely the Lord had mercy on me and did perfect the pot of beans that concerned me, and the children learned a tremendous lesson in trusting God.

7
No More Strength to Fight

Bending over to get an ice-cold soft drink from a shallow pool in the river, Joe's foot slipped on a rock; and he was quickly swept into "white water." He was on a rafting trip with a group of boys and their guides. They had stopped for lunch on the river bank and pulled off their cumbersome life jackets. White-water rafting is so much fun, and Joe, as most boys, loves excitement and speed.

The water swirled, twisted, and thrashed him against the rocks. He was trying with all his might to keep his head above the water. Fast water can be vicious, and it kept Joe's head under most of the time. A guide jumped into a kayak, hoping to intercept Joe, but both the kayak and Joe were traveling downstream at the same rate of speed. The other boys were running along the bank yelling and hoping to help. No one knows for sure exactly how far downstream Joe was swept, probably one half mile. The extreme cold temperature of the water brings on hypothermia quickly, and it had begun to set in. With his last ounce of strength, he tried to swim a few strokes toward the bank; the fight was over. A stranger risked his life to pull Joe out.

As I questioned Joe later for details, one sentence kept coming back to me. "Mom, I just gave up. I didn't have any more strength to fight." At that point God spared his

life in lieu of a better plan. He was only within a few seconds of drowning.

I believe people have to reach the same place in their spiritual walk. So often we, like the apostle Paul, kick against the Lord or we fight to do things our way. Some people try to work their way to salvation. Only when we finally give up fighting and struggling does God in His love reach down and pull us out just short of spiritual drowning. "For it is by grace you have been saved, through faith—and this not from yourselves, it is the gift of God—not by works, so that no one can boast" (Eph. 2:8-9, NIV).

8
Grasshoppers and the Tithe

Last summer, as I was examining some tender, young plants in my garden, I could feel my frustrations rising. The grasshoppers were still at it. Some plants were no longer recognizable, and many had been completely destroyed. I did not want to use commercial insecticides on my organic garden, but I couldn't see any other way. The friendly advice of our neighbors didn't work either.

In my total defeat, I looked to the promises from God's Word. I had heard there were at least 3,753 promises in the Bible, but I had claimed only about twenty-five of them. Was there one concerning grasshoppers? I checked in a little book *God's Promises Solve My Problems* by Glen Coon. However, this was no common problem, and the solution wasn't there. The only recourse was to search my Bible concordance. At last I found a text in Malachi 3:11; excitedly, I turned to it and read.

> I will rebuke the devourer for your sakes, and he shall not destroy the fruits of your ground; neither shall your vine cast her fruit before the time in the field, saith the Lord of hosts.

I reread verse 11 in the context of verse 10 to see what God's conditions were for His promise.

Bring ye all the tithes into the storehouse, that there may be meat in mine house, and prove me now herewith, saith the Lord of hosts, if I will not open you the windows of heaven, and pour you out a blessing, that there shall not be room enough to receive it.

As I read that verse, two words, "prove me," were impressed upon my heart. God would take care of the problem, if . . . Had we been faithful in bringing our tithes and offerings to God? I didn't honestly know for sure since my husband writes our tithe checks. I looked for Jim and asked him; he assured me we had been faithful. With joy in my heart, I went back to the garden and prayed, "God, we have kept our part of Your promise. Now I ask You to keep Your part. I believe in You and Your promises, and thank You in the name of Jesus for rebuking the devourer."

It didn't happen overnight, and I know God was testing my faith in His promise. Would I trust Him or poisonous spray to take care of the grasshoppers? Many times during the next few days I was tempted to take matters into my own hands, but I was always reminded that: "The Lord is not slow in keeping his promise, as some understand slowness. He is patient with you" (2 Pet. 3:9, NIV).

The tall grass around our garden was dry, and it became necessary for us to burn it. In so doing, 99 percent of the pests were destroyed. I'm glad I waited for God to "rebuke the devourer" His way. His bonus was a productive garden, not only for us but we had more than enough to share with friends throughout the summer.

God's promises really do solve my problems!

9
Dying to Live

It was fall, and I found myself in the vegetable garden harvesting potatoes. How well I remembered planting them only a few months earlier while falling snowflakes played on my hair. I had hoped for a bumper crop, and I was not disappointed. As I dug shovelful after shovelful of soft, rich earth, many potatoes came forth from their dark hiding places to lie beside others in my cardboard box.

I dug into one plant where I was sure I'd find more potatoes, only to find nothing but a thin, brown, wrinkled skin left from what I had originally planted. What had happened? Why hadn't it produced more potatoes?

While I turned this over in my mind, a thought in the Bible came into focus. Jesus had said, "Verily, verily, I say unto you, Except a corn of wheat fall into the ground and die, it abideth alone: but if it die, it bringeth forth much fruit" (John 12:24).

I felt He was speaking to me about dying to myself. Was I willing to die and bear much fruit for the kingdom of God, or would I choose to be selfish with my spiritual gifts and abide alone? I knew there was no joy in selfishness, but could I risk being ridiculed for Christ? I knew the answer, and I could only choose as the apostle Paul did when he testified,

I have been crucified with Christ and I no longer live, but Christ lives in me. The life I live in the body, I live by faith in the Son of God, who loved me and gave himself for me (Gal. 2:20, NIV)

After my decision, I prayed a new prayer: "Lord, help me die to self today so the living Christ will live His life in me and through me. I want to be the person You created me to be. Don't ever let me be selfish with what You have so freely and unselfishly given me."

Could I really have made any other decision when Jesus willingly died so I, His child, might be saved and bear much fruit for His kingdom?

10
The Good Shepherd

It was 1 AM; I had just settled down in my tent for a few hours of sleep. Hiking down Mount Ararat in the dark had brought about heavy fatigue.

I had camped in a small Turkish village surrounded by sleeping donkeys, goats, horses, dogs, and sheep. Suddenly the dogs began to bark. The sheep were frightened, stirring about and making peculiar noises. Two minutes later I heard a loud bang that sounded like a cannon. Whatever was the commotion? Soon one of our Turkish guides came to my tent, assuring me it was nothing more than a hungry wolf after a meal of mutton.

As I lay quietly in my sleeping bag, a shepherd appeared to quiet his sheep. I heard him begin his unusual lullaby: two soft, short whistles followed by a long one; two short, then a long. This strange whistling continued for twenty or thirty minutes. The quieting effect upon his sheep was amazing. They became absolutely still.

My mind wandered to the Good Shepherd and the many times He quiets His sheep. He also has a unique lullaby for us. The disciples heard it when Jesus came walking on the water toward their boat. His first words were, "Be of good cheer; it is I; be not afraid" (Matt. 14:27).

He still quiets our spirits today with those same words. Hebrews 13:5 has a promise from Him; He will never leave us or forsake us. With those sweet words singing in my head, I fell asleep.

11
Lessons from African Violets

African violets are not necessarily one of my favorite house plants. However, after more than twenty years of indoor gardening, I impetuously purchased a small one with large indigo flowers. For its special place of honor I chose what I thought was a most suitable spot with plenty of indirect lighting all day.

After two weeks it dropped its lovely blooms. I lovingly fed and watered it at regular intervals and waited for new blooms to appear. Month after month I continued caring for it—but still no new buds. *Maybe it would be happier in a different location with other plants,* I reasoned. *Perhaps it is lonely.* I moved it with the other plants and waited—still no blooms. I reread the instructions on the fertilizer box for the umpteenth time. By now more than a year had passed since the plant had bloomed. No plants rest that long. What could I be doing wrong? None of my other plants ever gave me that much trouble.

One day I decided to move the plant one more time to a different location where it had plenty of company and sunshine all day long. I fertilized the little monster again and watered it, then promptly forgot about it. A week or so later, as I was watering the others in the same area, I looked down to see this little violet in full bloom. "Well, praise the Lord" was my first reaction, then more

34

thoughtfully I wondered what I had done right or what I had done wrong all the other times. Never did I dream the Lord had a pointed lesson for me to learn.

The Holy Spirit brought to my memory this Scripture from the apostle Paul, "For I have learned, in whatsoever state I am, therewith to be content" (Phil. 4:11). I knew he was not referring to Colorado or Texas or any other state, but he was referring to whatever situation we find ourselves in to be content.

God was speaking to my heart: *Mary, that little plant is you. You should have bloomed in the Mojave desert where I planted you, but instead you complained. You could have bloomed in Houston, Texas, where I planted you, but you complained. It wasn't until I planted you in Colorado that you finally bloomed. Your attitudes prevented you from blooming for so many years. You could have given off the sweet fragrance of Jesus and had the beauty of His spirit for others to enjoy. See what you missed?*

My spirit was awfully grieved with this revelation. I knew He was right, and I had been so wrong. I repented on the spot and asked His cleansing forgiveness.

I may not always like the places He sends me, but with His help I will bloom where I am planted so I may say with Paul, "I have learned in whatsoever state I am, therewith to be content."

12
Lessons from Seashells

One afternoon during our stay in South Africa we had an hour break from our schedule, so we walked down to the shore to relax and look for shells. We saw a working-man there, gathering trash from the beach and putting it into a large bag. As we approached him, I asked if he'd seen any shells along the water's edge that morning. No, he hadn't. Those were his only words.

That meant the shells must be scarce, and it would be difficult to find any during our brief walk. Yet a short time later, we returned to the hotel with a handful of beautiful shells we had found simply by being alert for them.

How could that man not have seen the shells as he walked the shore for hours searching the sand? Had he grown so absorbed with looking for waste and debris that he'd stopped taking notice of the shells? Was he no longer able to see their delicate colors sparkling under a thin veil of sand and water?

It was a small incident. More likely the man regarded us as tourists and didn't want to encourage any more questions from us. Pondering over his answer, I saw Christ's object lesson for me. I thought of 2 Corinthians 3:18:

But we all, with open face beholding as in a glass the glory
of the Lord, are changed into the same image from glory
to glory, even as by the Spirit of the Lord.

Here the apostle Paul was explaining how Christians
turn to the Lord and become filled with His Spirit. In this
way, they are made in the image of the Lord, and their
own lives reflect His glory and beauty.

But even more basically, I believe the Lord is telling us
we are all reflections of our inner spirits. All that we read;
all that we listen to; all that we think, do, and say is food
for our spirits. What we choose to feed our spirits will
determine what we become.

If we constantly take in things that are impure, un-
healthy, or unhappy, that will be the image we reflect.
Yet, if we desire to control our intake and concern ourselves with what is good and pure, we will become a reflection of those things.

In these times, that struggle is especially hard. There
is the temptation to look upon the foul, the violent, the
coarse, and the dishonest things of this world with too
much relish. Soon everything we do or think seems to
take on the shadow of worldliness and unholiness.

Yet, for our own well-being, God has commanded us to
seek out the good and the righteous:

Fix your thoughts on what is true and good and right.
Think about things that are pure and lovely, and dwell on
the fine, good things in others. Think about all you can
praise God for and be glad about (Phil. 4:8, TLB).

Concentrating on the good may not eliminate the bad.
But by becoming filled with the Lord's Spirit and per-
meating your mind with His Word, you can be lifted
above the things of this world.

Keep looking for the lovely shells along the beach, Concentrate on the pure and beautiful things in your friends, your job, and every area of your life. Search for them, and they will multiply within your gaze, giving you new eyes with which to look upon the world. Give yourself to the things that are good, and your life will become great.

13
Nagging and the Jay

Squawk! The Pinon jay was at it again for the umpteenth time that day. Our poor mama cat seemed to get no peace from her tormentor. As a matter of fact, the bird's constant squawking was getting on my nerves, too.

I could not figure out why that bird would not leave the cat alone: the cat was sleeping peacefully on the redwood deck, not pestering anyone or anything.

The bird sat on the porch railing and squawked, then she'd jump within inches of mama cat's nose or tail and screech some more, steal a few pieces of cat food, and jump back onto the railing once again.

As the same scene occurred time after time and day after day, I often watched in amazement. Finally, when the cat could take no more, she would either beg to come in or hide away from her tormentor.

It didn't take long for me to understand the meaning of what was going on. That little Pinon jay was a reminder to me of my relationship to my family. It's so easy to get caught up in the frustrations of rearing a family and being a homemaker to the extent that a woman lashes out at those whom she loves most of all. God was speaking to me as a wife and mother that day.

As the tears began to flow from my eyes, I remembered the verse of Scripture in Proverbs about a woman causing strife in her home. I knew this verse well since I had recently read several other verses on the same subject.

Proverbs 19:13; 21:9; and 27:15-16 all say about the same thing:

> A constant dripping on a rainy day and a cranky woman are much alike! You can no more stop her complaints than you can stop the wind or hold onto anything with oil-slick hands (vv. 15-16, TLB).

In spite of the tears, I thanked God for the spiritual insight He gave me that day by opening my eyes through a bird. It's funny. The birds still come back, but they don't pester the cat anymore.

14
Truths from Shiny Strawberries

The aroma of fresh strawberries on the vine was a reminder that they must be picked before the first snowfall. I had promised myself to pick them that very afternoon.

A few hours later I was among the thick, lush, green leaves in my garden with fifteen rows of strawberries to pick. My back ached just thinking about the project. I knelt and began to fill my large metal bowl with delicious red berries. As I picked, I also had to discern which should be picked and which should be left. I wanted only the firm ones for freezing and making jam. Being selective, I began to notice the firmer ones were highly glossed while the others had already begun to lose their luster. I wondered why. Were they past their peak of usefulness? Was their dullness a signal to leave them on the vine to rot? I left them. Was there perhaps a spiritual correlation between the dull strawberries and a Christian's life?

I remembered Moses and how his face shone with the glory of God after he had encountered Him on Mount Sinai. Why had the glow left Moses' face? He had not been filled with the Holy Spirit and therefore could not reflect the glory of Jesus. The glory of God upon his face lasted only a short while.

> For what was glorious has no glory now in comparison with the surpassing glory. And if what was fading away came with glory, how much greater is the glory of that which lasts! Therefore, since we have such a hope, we are very bold. We are not like Moses, who would put a veil over his face to keep the Israelites from gazing at it while the radiance was fading away (2 Cor. 3:10-13, NIV).

Verse 18 reads,

> And we, who with unveiled faces all reflect the Lord's glory, are being transformed into his likeness with ever-increasing glory, which comes from the Lord, who is the Spirit.

The shiny strawberries had indeed revealed a spiritual truth to me. Since I belong to Jesus, and He belongs to me, I should reflect His glory, His image, and all that He is. If I am not reflecting who He is, there is probably unconfessed sin in my life that needs to be made right. My wish is to reflect always the person of Jesus in my life, so I may shine with the countenance of His glory.

15
The Peerless Leader

Wild horses, I am told, always have a stallion as their leader. During bitter-cold winter months, the herd often turns its backs on the biting wind, and they search for shelter. The shelter they choose could mean their death if they allow themselves to become trapped by heavy snows with no source of food or water.

When the herd begins to head toward disaster, the stallion instinctively senses it and rears up with his mane shaking and nostrils snorting, sounding the danger signal. The herd responds faithfully, even if it means it must turn directly into the wind to follow their peerless leader. They believe he will lead them to safety.

I am comforted by knowing that our Savior offers perfect leadership and security to the flock which follows Him. Even when the path we are walking seems logical and safe, we must be open to God's direction.

Lord, build in us the kind of faith that will allow us to follow You always, even if we must leave the path of least resistance and walk directly into the storm. You always promise to answer our faith with Your guidance.

Trust in the Lord with all your heart,
And do not lean on your own understanding.
In all your ways acknowledge Him,
And He will make your paths straight (Prov. 3:5-6,
NASB).

16
Not Seeing but Believing

When a blind person passes by, I always watch with amazement and wonder. Amazement because I have never seen one unsure of a footstep while using a walking stick or a guide dog.

I chanced to meet such a person and her dog one evening after a church service. Her face glowed with the Spirit of God; she was radiant inside and out. She seemed only to see others with her heart.

After that encounter, I wondered aloud what incredible faith blind persons must have. Faith that someone won't hit them with a bicycle or car while they are walking, that their dogs will never cross the street on a red light and will always protect them from danger. Since they cannot walk by sight, they are compelled to walk by trust.

The apostle Paul defined *faith* in Hebrews 11:1: "Now faith is being sure of what we hope for and certain of what we do not see" (NIV).

Remember when Christ appeared to His disciples after His resurrection but Thomas was not present? The others reported to him that they had seen the Lord. Thomas said that he would not believe them until he saw for himself the nail prints and thrust his hand into the side of Jesus. After eight days, Jesus appeared to them again and Thomas was present. He gave Thomas permission to go ahead, touch the nail prints, and put his hand into His side. Thomas may have done that. We really don't know. Then he cried aloud, "My Lord and my God!" Jesus then gave him a gentle correction. "Thomas, because you have seen Me, you have believed: blessed are they that have not seen, and yet have believed" (John 20: 24-29, author's paraphrase).

We seem to become so discouraged and depressed when we can't see God doing something in our lives or the lives of our loved ones like we think He should. We become gloomy when we don't see a promise in His Word materialize as quickly as we think it should. We need to remember Jesus' words to Thomas and know He is developing a strong place in the weak spot of our characters by teaching us to trust and lean on Him totally while He leads us through the dark tunnels of life. He promised in Matthew 28:20: "Lo, I am with you alway, even unto the end of the world" (Matt. 28:20).

17
Climbing Higher

I'm pressing on the upward way,
New heights I'm gaining ev'ry day;
Still praying as I onward bound,
Lord, plant my feet on higher ground.
I want to scale the utmost height
And catch a gleam of glory bright;
But still I'll pray till heav'n I've found,
"Lord, lead me on to higher ground."
—Johnson Oatman, Jr.

The words from this precious old hymn were echoing in my thoughts today as I was climbing on Barr Trail that leads to the summit of Pikes Peak. Each time I hike, I go a little farther, a little higher, always onward toward the goal. I climb for ten or fifteen minutes, then rest for one minute, conditioning my heart rate for a return trip to Mount Ararat. During those brief stops, I gaze eastward toward the horizon; the higher I climb, the more spectacular the view. I look down to the parking lot below, and there sits my little blue Volkswagen; now it seems like it is only one centimeter in length.

The higher we climb with Jesus, the smaller and farther away cares seem to be. Sometimes the trail becomes steep, rocky, and almost impossible to climb; but Jesus is always there to lend us His hand and give us a firm foothold. David the psalmist wrote in Psalm 18:33: "He maketh my feet like hinds' feet, and setteth me upon my high places."

The longer our feet travel the pathway, the more sure-footed we become. We need to look ahead one step at a time toward the summit and only stop for a brief moment to catch our breath and see how far we have come. "I press toward the mark for the prize of the high calling of God in Christ Jesus" (Phil. 3:14).

18
Divine Molding

"Sand Molds." What are they? The next time you are walking along the seashore, stop and look behind you. You will have made a simple sand mold with your foot-prints. If the sand is mixed with clay and has become cold, settled, and hard-packed, the ground may break and crumble under your weight. If the ground is very hard, your foot may not make a print at all. Others who come along behind you won't even know that you've walked before them. But if you walk close to the water's edge where the sand is moist and loose, it will gently ooze up between your toes, making a cushion for your feet. Your foot-prints will sink deep into the sand, and those who follow you will clearly see that someone else has walked that ground.

People can be like sand beside the sea. If their character and personality have been hardened, if their habits, purposes, and beliefs have deeply settled into a strict way of life, they may crumble and break under the weight of God as He tries to mold their shape and form. If their hearts have been deeply hardened, God may not be able to make the slightest imprint on their stubborn lives. Others may not see even a trace that God has struggled for their lives.

Those who believe that Jesus Christ is the Savior and

Son of God are commanded to give up their hardened life-styles, to lose their pride and stubbornness, and to give up all rights to their own lives. God's guidance and direction are accepted as wiser than their own. They become as moist sand along the water's edge, responding to God's every touch, reflecting His image. Onlookers can't help seeing the imprints of compassion, joy, and peace in the Christian character and knowing that God has passed through this life before them. In order for the molder to transform hard, crumbling clay into soft, pliable materials for making useful and gorgeous pots, he must have water. For God to transform hard, bitter people into responsive, trusting students of His Word, He must have their consent—an act of their wills.

Hannah Whitall Smith, in *A Christian's Secret for a Happy Life,* described a man's will as "not the wish of the man, or even his purpose, but the deliberate choice, the deciding power, the king, to which all that is in the man must yield obedience. . . . It is not the feelings of the man God wants, but the man himself."

It is not easy for a person to give up his will to God, but it is the only way the Lord can mold His child to perfection. And just as the potter must fire his clay if it is to hold its shape for a lifetime, so the Lord must put His followers through difficult trials if they are to achieve and maintain a more Christlike character. He will demand that they love when they feel like hating, that they give when they expect to receive, and that they stand firm in the faith that His molding is not accidental but divine. "Behold, as the clay is in the potter's hand, so are ye in mine hand" (Jer. 18:6).

If we will only obey God's command and present ourselves to Him as a living sacrifice, He has promised to take possession of our surrendered wills and begin immediately to work in us "that which is well-pleasing in his sight, through Jesus Christ" (Heb. 13:21), giving us the mind that was in Christ and transforming us into His image.

19
Rebirth

Spring is a time for buds to emerge from the trees and birds to reappear on the branches. These past months I've seen the gray winter steadily disappear. I've watched carefully the dark, somber-looking cocoons that have slept through the cold respond to the warming rays of the sun. Finally, butterflies have burst through, overflowing with vibrant color and new life.

The human spirit can be like a cocoon wrapped up inside itself, deadened to the life surrounding it, unaware of the potential beauty bound up within that needs only a catalyst to trigger the miracle of new creation.

The catalyst for a butterfly cocoon is the penetrating heat of the spring sun. For the dark and sullen human spirit, it is the warmth of the Son of God, Jesus Christ. As His warmth and strength penetrate into our beings, miracles of new creation begin to take place. God promises this new life to those who have accepted His Son, Jesus, as their Lord and Savior (2 Cor. 5:17)

Therefore if any man be in Christ, he is a new creature: old things are passed away; behold, all things are become new.

The grace of God not only justifies but also makes "a new

creation" which results in a changed style of life (v. 15, *The Ryrie Study Bible*, Chicago: Moody Press, 1976).

Rebirth is not an easy concept to understand. In John 3, Nicodemus was having problems understanding the meaning of being reborn. If anyone should have understood it would have been Nicodemus. He was a member of the Sanhedrin, a learned select group of "spiritual" leaders of his time. Jesus said to him:

"I tell you the truth, unless a man is born again, he cannot see the kingdom of God." "How can a man be born when he is old?" Nicodemus asked. "Surely he cannot enter a second time into his mother's womb to be born!" Jesus answered, "I tell you the truth, unless a man is born of water and the Spirit, he cannot enter the kingdom of God. Flesh gives birth to flesh, but the Spirit gives birth to spirit (John 3:3-6, NIV).

We can only reproduce human life, but the Holy Spirit gives new life from heaven.

Life without Christ is like living within a cocoon. But just as the butterfly breaks out of its darkness, so can we be reborn in the Spirit and find new freedom from sin. Come and be free in the living sunshine of Jesus Christ our Lord.

20
Don't Squeeze!

How many times have you held in your hands a tiny, new, soft, baby chicken so trusting and fragile? I was not reared on a farm, but we had enough room to allow Mother to raise a few chickens. When I was a small child, Mother had a large cardboard box with a small light bulb overhead for warmth. It was filled with new, baby chicks. Sometimes Mother would allow me to hold one of those precious, yellow-feathered balls in my hand. I wanted to pour out all of my love to it by squeezing and stroking its head. The chick did not enjoy my type of love, so it began to struggle frantically for freedom from its pain. It peeped loudly. It was trying to tell me, "Please be careful; I am very delicate, and you are hurting me."

The decision was difficult. I could do one of two things to show my true feelings of love. I could squeeze tighter and cause injury or death—a selfish love, or I could let the chick go free and live—an unselfish love. The chicken's life was in my hands—the choice was mine.

This little story gives insight into those I love, especially my children whom God has entrusted to me. His instruction is to train our children in His ways of truth and light; then when they grow older they will not depart from those teachings. We make unwise choices as children and as adults, and we must suffer the consequences (see Prov. 22:6). Sometimes a spanking is part of their instruction, if not from the parents, then from the Father who teaches us His ways (see Prov. 29:15). Let us take our child training joyfully, as well as seriously, by remembering discipline, love our children unselfishly, teach them of God's ways, then let go of them and let God have His way in their lives.

Correct your son, and he will give you comfort;
He will also delight your soul (Prov. 29:17, NASB).

21
The Shepherd's Voice

Most of you have seen the picture of the Good Shepherd holding a little lamb. I'd like to share the story of that picture as it was once told me.

The Loving Shepherd leads his flock in green pastures and beside still waters. Sometimes there is a new lamb that does not follow the flock and continues to stray, bringing anxiety to the Shepherd.

It has not learned the sound of the master's voice; therefore, when it is called, it pays no attention.

The only way to get a straying lamb's attention is to teach it a harsh, yet loving lesson. The shepherd will break its front legs, thereby forcing the lamb to be carried. Tenderly, the shepherd carries the suffering lamb while he talks to it and strokes it.

When its legs are healed, the lamb is put back with the flock. Now when the shepherd speaks, it will no longer stray. For the little one has learned the sound of its master's voice and comes when it is called.

The Bible tells us about sheep who run off and get lost and also about those who hear His voice and don't run away. "All we like sheep have gone astray; we have turned every one to his own way" (Isa. 53:6).

A friend once asked, "How do I know the voice of God? How do I know if it is my own thoughts, Satan's, or God's?

The Bible explains:

He that entereth in by the door is the shepherd of the
sheep. To him the porter openeth; and the sheep hear his
voice; and he calleth his own sheep by name, and leadeth
them out. And when he putteth forth his own sheep, he
goeth before them, and the sheep follow him: for they
know his voice. And a stranger will they not follow, but
will flee from him: for they know not the voice of strangers
(John 10:2-5).

If you cannot discern the voice of God, perhaps you are
not His sheep or you are not listening to His voice.

My sheep hear my voice, and I know them, and they follow
me: And I give unto them eternal life; and they shall
never perish, neither shall any man pluck them out of my
hand (John 10:27-28).

Train your spirit to know the voice of the Shepherd.
After your prayer time, linger awhile before the throne
and listen with your heart to the voice of the Shepherd.
Soon you will recognize His voice.

22
Missy Came Back

His name was Charlie and her's was Missy. They were a pair of hamsters given to our children around the Christmas holidays. We spent hours watching their antics: housekeeping, nest building, and raising one litter after another. The female was exceptionally loving and never bit any of us; we couldn't say the same about her mate.

In the summer, we placed their cage on the screened-in porch to keep them safe from the neighboring cats. Unfortunately, someone forgot to close and lock the cage door after playing with them one day. Joy came running to me nearly in tears. Charlie had fallen more than three feet and was dead on the concrete floor. Surely the mate must be close by and also dead. We searched high and low, but no Missy was found.

I kept having this inward feeling that she was still alive and running around. But how could she survive more than a few days without being fed? She didn't know how to forage. I suggested to Joy we should pray about it on the spot and believe that God would return Missy to her.

Days went by, and the empty cage was a constant reminder of sadness. We continued to pray and believe that God would bring that small, insignificant hamster back to us. As days turned into weeks, it was easy to forget the little animal; but the feeling of Missy's return persisted. I knew she was alive and expected her to return someday.

One day the neighbor children told Joy they had seen a hamster running down the curb and gutter and suggested it might be Missy. The children raced to me in excitement, "Mom, do you think it's Missy?" "I don't know, but get a small trash can and a pair of gloves. If it's she, she will be wild and may bite you." Grabbing the nearest trash can, they breathlessly slammed out the back door. I stood there in awe and wonder as the reassuring Scripture from Jeremiah 32:27 came back to me. "Behold, I am the Lord, the God of *all* flesh: is there any thing too hard for me?" (author's italics). *No, Lord,* I thought, *nothing is ever too difficult for You.* I knew before I ever saw the little creature that He had indeed sent Missy home. She had been missing one month. The Creator had watched over and fed her, then at the precise time sent her back home. We gathered to thank God for His goodness and answered prayer.

Yes, she was a mess of scruffy fur with all four feet abcessed, not to mention the absence of toenails. We nursed her back to health with antibiotics and wholesome food. You might think it nonsense to take up God's time with such a foolish request. His time is more valuable than wasting it on some little kid's lost rodent.

The Bible says, "Not one sparrow . . . can fall to the ground without your Father knowing it" (Matt. 10:29, TLB). A fallen bird is not the issue here. The infinite importance of man versus animals is what God wants us to understand. If a child's lost hamster was important to God, then we as His children are vastly more important to Him. "But the very hairs of your head are all numbered. Fear ye not therefore, ye are of more value than many sparrows," (Matt. 10:30-31).

Thanks be to God the Creator for the importance He places on us, His children. Not only are the hairs of our head numbered but also He knows us by our names. In John 10:3, we, His children, are called sheep: "and *he calleth his own* sheep *by name*" (author's italics). Isn't it wonderful? He knows us, loves us, has redeemed us, and wants to have a relationship with us. Is there anything too hard for Him?

23
Approaching with Confidence

Christmas of 1972 was extra special to our family. We were in the Holy Land for a television special where Jim shared the story of the birth of Jesus Christ with thousands on Christmas Eve. We had a large choir traveling with us which performed Handel's *Messiah* on the same program. What an awesome experience!

The next day we left Israel for Jordan. Jim requested an audience with King Hussein to present him the flag of Jordan which Jim had flown to the moon. The king was on his honeymoon we were told, so he probably wouldn't see us. However, he was informed of the concert and Jim's speaking that evening in the music hall where the choir once again would be performing Handel's *Messiah*.

The king and his queen decided to attend, and his staff called it a "command performance." A few of the adults were invited to sit in the king's viewing box with him and his wife. The children were to sit with some of the tour group.

The program was proceeding exceedingly well. King Hussein and Queen Alia were listening with rapt attention. Suddenly, out of nowhere, our seven-year-old Jan appeared. She sneaked into my lap to whisper, "I need to go potty." I was amazed! The king's viewing box was heavily guarded. How did she get past all of those guards?

Looking back on that experience, I am reminded of how many times I, too, come into the presence of my Heavenly King. Unlike Jan who came quietly into the king's presence, I came boldly. Often I come sobbing and crying out the name of Jesus. I know He hears me coming a long way off as I approach His throne room. He probably has a smile on His face and is thinking, *Here she comes again.* Fortunately, Jesus understands me and cares.

The Bible says:

> We do not have a high priest who is unable to sympathize with our weaknesses, but we have one who has been tempted in every way, just as we are—yet was without sin. Let us then approach the throne of grace with confidence, so that we may receive mercy and find grace to help us in our time of need (Heb. 4:15-16, NIV).

What a joy and privilege to experience coming boldly before the throne of grace, knowing my King will always have His arms outstrectched in love to me. Matthew 18 tells us that when we come before God we must come as a little child—*humble.* Jesus said, "All that the Father gives me will come to me, and whoever comes to me I will never drive away" (John 6:37, NIV).

Thanks be to God I can come joyfully into His presence.

24
Flood My Riverbed

Our first well was shallow, but we had sweet, clear water. After two years of constant use by a family of seven, it dribbled to a halt. We were faced with drilling a new and deeper well.

The first two tries ended with the well collapsing at two hundred feet. We were hoping for success on the third try. After drilling four or five hundred feet, they hit a marvelous water flow and hooked it up to the house. Our rejoicing was short-lived. The water tasted, looked, and felt terrible; its mineral content and hardness were the worst in the valley. The coloring was somewhere between red-orange and brown. We even felt yuckie after taking a shower, and our hair felt like a scouring pad after a shampoo. What could we do before the bad water ruined all our plumbing? We could drink bottled water and I could take the laundry to the laundromat, but that still wouldn't solve the problem. We could dig another expensive well, but the chances were we would hit more of the same bad water. Our only choice was to tap into city water. It would be costly, but we were willing to pay the price for clean, clear, sweet water.

The Samaritan woman at Jacob's well was willing to pay the price. Jesus asked her for a drink of water while He sat and visited with her. She seemed so overcome by the fact a Jew would talk to a half-breed Samaritan that she forgot to give Him the drink He requested. He told her that if she only knew to whom she was speaking she would have asked *Him* for a drink, and He would have given her living water.

> "Whosoever drinks the water I give him will never thirst. Indeed, the water I give him will become in him a spring of water welling up to eternal life."
> The woman said to him, "Sir, give me this water so that I won't get thirsty and have to keep coming here to draw water" (John 4:14-15, NIV).

I can almost see the wheels turning in her head, *Sure, mister, I'll gladly drink your kind of water. Then I won't have to drag these heavy water pots around anymore. They're so heavy it gives me a stiff neck and sore back nearly everyday.*

Jesus never once judged or criticized her, even though she was living in sin. He simply continued to hold forth the cup of "living water" for her to drink. She began to perceive He was a holy man of God. Then Jesus told her He was the Messiah. She accepted the cup of living water and drank deeply. That simple act of drinking from the living well converted nearly a whole city.

Jesus beckons to us today: "If any man thirst, let him come unto me, and drink. He that believeth on me, as the scripture hath said, out of his belly shall flow rivers of living water" (John 7:37-38).

Like the woman at the well, we often come asking Jesus to fill our cups. But when we take an inward spiritual inventory, we realize that one sip or one cup of that wonderful water isn't enough. We long for more until we cry out, "Lord, flood my riverbed." We must be utterly saturated with the living water until it spills over and drips from us onto all those with whom we come in contact. Fellow Christians, as we walk and live in this world, be filled with the Spirit of the Living Water; only then will we make an impact for Jesus.

25
Brokenness and Blessing

In India the narrow, dusty streets of the marketplace are lined with clay pots and others wares for sale. The clay pots are used for storing oil, flour, and various other perishables, and for carrying water. When walking in the market area, one sees women carrying containers upon their heads. Many times the water containers are earthen vessels.

I could not look at one of those pots without remembering how we too, as God's children, are clay in the Potter's hands (Isa. 64:8). When the potter finishes the pottery he sets it aside to dry and to be fired at a high temperature. Only then can it be used for a container.

Some people fill their containers with the garbage of this world, such as bitterness, hatred, wrath, lust, and greed. The list goes on and on. Others fill theirs with fruit like joy, peace, long-suffering, meekness, love, gentleness, faith, goodness, and temperance (Gal. 5:22-23). With what have we filled our vessels? What will come tumbling out when our clay pots are broken? The answer is obvious: Whatever was in the pot will come out. If our vessels contain the diamond-like treasure of Jesus Christ, who will ever see its many-faceted brilliance unless the pot is broken?

I like Watchman Nee's explanation of this principle in his book *The Release of the Spirit:*

> So the Treasure is in the earthen vessel, but if the earthen vessel is not broken, who can see the Treasure within? What is the final objective of the Lord's working in our lives? It is to break this earthen vessel, to break our alabaster box, to crack open our shell. The Lord longs to find a way to bless the world through those who belong to Him. Brokenness is the way of blessing, the way of fragrance, the way of fruitfulness, but it is also a path sprinkled with blood. Yes, there is blood from many wounds. When we offer ourselves to the Lord to be at His service, we cannot afford to be lenient, to spare ourselves. We must allow the Lord utterly to crack our outward man, so that He may find a way for His out-working.

The striking force to one's earthen vessel is an act of one's will. When a person finally becomes willing for God to break him, then the brilliance of Jesus Christ will shine forth to illuminate the pathway for others. The key to brokenness is a willing spirit, willing to be corrected and taught by the Holy Spirit. The question we must ask ourselves is, Am I willing? If the answer up to now has been no, may I suggest it may be the problem addressed in 1 Samuel 15:23: "Rebellion is as the sin of witchcraft, and stubbornness is as iniquity and idolatry."

If the answer is yes, it is because of Philippians 2:13 (NIV): "It is God who works in you to will and to act according to his good purpose." An earthen vessel is indeed a special treasure to God.

26
Burden Bearers

"Mommmmm!" The agonized scream of my child pierced my ears from the opposite side of the soccer field. The referee blew hard on his whistle, and the game stopped, leaving the players in suspended animation.

In seconds I was kneeling by Jan's side as she writhed in agony. "I heard it pop, Mom, I heard it pop" was all she could say. Others standing near her nodded in agreement. They had heard it too. We gently lifted Jan into our car and drove to the nearest hospital. Her statement was confirmed by X-rays. She had indeed heard the "pop." Both bones in the lower part of her leg were fractured.

The spirit of her teammates had been fractured too, and they were hurting emotionally for their fallen member. After the game, most of the girls came to the hospital emergency room just to let Jan know they cared. In spite of her pain, she was encouraged.

In the apostle Paul's letter to the Galatians, he admonished the Christians to "bear ye one another's burdens, and so fulfil the law of Christ" (6:2). *Ellicott's Commentary on the Whole Bible*, volume 4, explains it this way:

> Bear ye one another's burdens. Take them upon yourselves by kindly sympathy. Our Lord Himself was said to

"bear" the physical infirmities of those whom He healed. (Matthew 8:17), "He bore our sickness.")

The meaning is that "By showing sympathy to others in their distress, of whatever kind that distress may be— whether physical, mental, or moral—the Christian will best fulfill that "new commandment" bequeathed to him by his Master, the "law of love." (See John 13:34; I John 3:23.)

In other words, Christians, care enough to become involved with someone else's hurts and pain, and thereby you will fulfill the law of love. When someone knows you care enough to be involved, their burden is far easier for them to carry.

What a wonderful God we have—he is the Father of our Lord Jesus Christ, the source of every mercy, and the one who so wonderfully comforts and strengthens us in our hardships and trials. And why does he do this? So that when others are troubled, needing our sympathy and encouragement, we can pass on to them this same help and comfort God has given us (2 Cor. 1:3-4, TLB).

27
Playing Without Power

Michael is a German boy who is a marvelous musician; he plays the electric guitar. He was part of the instrumental accompaniment for the *Word of Life* men's quartet in Germany. The quartet always sang before my husband Jim brought the message of the evening. That particular night Michael was playing with gusto and putting himself into his music. His face reflected pure concentration. When the music was finished, Michael bent down to unplug his guitar only to find out what I had already observed. His instrument hadn't even been plugged in! In spite of Michael's fervent playing, the guitar made no sound. Poor Michael was so embarrassed, and I could feel his embarrassment as color rose in his cheeks.

Immediately, I saw an object lesson in this incident. I asked Michael if I could share the story the following night in another town and promised not to use his name. He agreed.

You see, so often Christians are in high gear to serve the Lord, and yet their efforts fall flat. Perhaps they run ahead of God in their eagerness to share, and they fail. Their ministry may have no power and bear no fruit. These problems can quickly discourage a Christian. Let's take a closer look into the problems and see what the root cause may be. Isaiah 59:2 (TLB) says: "The trouble is that your sins have cut you off from God. Because of sin he has turned his face away from you and will not listen anymore."

Unconfessed sin in our lives grieves the Holy Spirit of God so much that He doesn't want to watch us sin. Sin disconnects us from the power source; therefore, it is expedient that we keep short accounts in the sin department. We must not pile up our sins before a righteous God because they will testify against us. We must repent and confess our sin immediately—then our relationship with the Father is restored. Only then will we be plugged into the source of power. This incredible power is what makes our service to God effective and a constant source of joy. This power brings boldness into our ministry and bears much fruit for the kingdom of God. The Holy Spirit's power enables us to walk with God instead of running ahead or lagging behind.

Zechariah 4:6 tells us how we can have a successful walk with God:

> "Not by might [our strength], nor by power [our power], but by my Spirit, says the Lord of Hosts—you will succeed because of my Spirit, though you are few and weak" (TLB).

In John 6:63 Jesus said, "The Spirit gives life; the flesh counts for nothing. The words I have spoken to you are spirit and they are life" (NIV).

To experience life to its fullest and best, we need to stop running around with our electrical cords unplugged and dragging behind us. Let's pick up the cord and plug it into the Source of power, the Holy Spirit of God, and experience a refreshingly new walk with God.

28
The Fizzled-out Experiment

In December 1983, Jim and I were featured speakers in a four-day revival at Whiteman Air Force Base, Missouri.

The first evening I shared many events of forgiven sins in my life. I wanted to end the talk with Isaiah 1:18 and a demonstration of how quickly God forgives confessed sin. I had two clear glass tumblers, both half full of water; I then added a heaping tablespoon of a red-colored commercial drink in each glass to represent sin: "though your sins be as scarlet." To the first glass I added a dry blueing bleach that the manufacturer said "will do the job." The only thing that happened was that the water turned red blue. It reminded me so much of what the world says to do when we have problems or sin in our lives. It says, "Pretend it doesn't exist, color it blue, gloss it over, call it deviant behavior, seek a phycoanalyst to tell you 'it's normal since everyone is doing it,'" and a hundred other remedies that won't work.

Into the second glass of red water, I added a small amount of bleaching chemical, expecting it to clear within ten seconds. Nothing happened! I read on: "They shall be as white as snow; though they be red like crimson, they shall be as wool." I added more of the powerful bleaching agent and continued to stir. The congregation sat spellbound waiting for the color to disappear. Absolutely nothing happened. I had done that exact experiment at least

74

seventy-five times, and it had never failed. I must admit I certainly was flustered. Concluding my talk, I assured the people that Jesus never fails: He "is the same yesterday and today and forever" (Heb. 13:8, NIV) and He always forgives confessed sin (1 John 1:9). Even if my experiment did fail, He never does. I sat down.

My face felt flushed with embarrassment over my failure, and my mind would not let me forget the fizzled-out experiment. When the meeting was over, we tried it again. Again it failed. I blamed it on the high mineral content of the water and tried to dismiss it from my mind.

The man who lent me his chemical was convinced it was a bad batch since the same experiment had failed for him too. He went home and found a new, unopened bottle and tried the experiment again. It worked. So, what had messed us up was a bad bottle of chemicals, perhaps too old, which had lost all of its strength.

I was still pondering over the lesson the Lord was teaching me. Yes, I had learned one. When all else fails, Jesus doesn't; but there was more, then it dawned.

> Faith by itself, if it is not accompanied by action, is dead. But someone will say, "You have faith; I have deeds." Show me your faith without deeds, and I will show you my faith by what I do (Jas. 2:17-18, NIV).

The red-colored drink was faith by itself; the inert chemical was dead works, and it was able to change nothing. On the other hand, the new chemicals added to the red water got results. That is faith with works. There is an act and a reaction. Faith with works is powerful when used, and lives become changed.

I'd far rather be a new and potent bottle of chemicals for Jesus Christ, and put my faith into action, than be a fizzled-out experiment for the world.

29
Make a Sign!

Big dump trucks had been roaring up our private drive for days, stirring up the dust. Upon nearing the house, the drivers would suddenly realize *Oops, wrong road,* then begin backing down and turning into the field where Jim had planted many tiny pine trees. The new neighbor's road is twenty-five feet from ours, and they were beginning to build their new house.

I could see many huge tire tracks where Jim's little trees were pushed into the earth. I know how carefully he plants new ones each year and how tenderly he cares for and waters them. I also knew that if he saw what I had seen he would become very upset. My thought processes began to work overtime. Perhaps I could sow nails, tacks, and other sharp objects that might flatten tires in the field. Then again maybe a nice roll of barbed wire would be enough to entangle the trucks. I was desperate to get the drivers' attention. I had already spoken to some of the drivers about the trees, but I wasn't willing to spend my days directing traffic to the right road.

I suspected the enemy was doing his tactics on us since our new neighbors are not Christians, and the devil would have us be enemies.

Somewhere in my thoughts began to materialize the Scripture from Matthew 5:9, "Blessed are the peacemakers." Okay, God, how do I make a peaceable situation out of this? The thought came immediately: *People do read signs, you know.* Oh yes, how come I hadn't thought of it? A sign. Yes, I could manage that. I found an old board 18 by 20 inches, looked until I found an old paint brush and some white paint, and began my project. The difficult part was trying to find the electric drill to make holes through the sign for attaching it to the post.

I stood back to admire my work—not professional, but I was sure it would do the trick. It had one word and three numbers boldly painted in dark blue: IRWIN 480. I took the new sign along with the sledge hammer and found just the right spot at the beginning of our drive and pounded it into place. All that was left was for me to wait.

Amazing! Not another stray dump truck has come down our road, not one ugly word or deed has been spoken or done.

Jesus didn't make a mistake when He said, "Blessed are the peacemakers: for they shall be called the children of God" (Matt. 5:9).

30
Jesus Removes the Stingers

Our Joey was an inquisitive, busy nine-year-old. Since school was out for the summer, he had plenty of time to find trouble.

I saw him running up the driveway as fast as his little legs could carry him and hollering, "Mom!" I met him at the front door, and with nary a tear he told me the bees had stung him.

He had been wandering on our eight acres and came upon his dad's beehive. It had been there for several years without being robbed of honey, and none of us knew for sure whether the bees still inhabited the hive. Seeing no activity around the hive he decided to kick it just to find out if maybe one bee were still around. You can guess the rest of the story. He soon realized he was no match for the bees; I took him into the bathroom under a bright light and began to pull out all of the stingers. After they were removed, we made a paste of baking soda and water and applied it to all of the swelling sting marks. Joe is fifteen now, and that experience has left a lasting impression.

As I was running it through my memory the other day, a Scripture popped into my mind: "O death, where is they sting? O grave, where is thy victory?" (1 Cor. 15:55).

It is painful to lose a loved one in death. I know. I lost my kid brother fifteen years ago in a climbing accident.

It did hurt, it did sting, and I did cry a lot. The separation was painful for a while. God in His love for me reached down with His tweezers and removed the stingers and dried my tears. It doesn't hurt anymore.

When Jesus returns to take the saved home with Him our bodies will be changed into His likeness and we shall exchange our mortality for immortality and death *will* be swallowed up in victory (1 Cor. 15:52).

God shall wipe away all tears from their eyes; and there shall be no more death, neither sorrow, nor crying, neither shall there be any more pain: for the former things are passed away (Rev. 21:4).

What a precious promise! Jesus really is the stinger remover.

31
Angel in the Chasm

There is a way which seems right to a man,
But its end is the way of death" (Prov. 14:12, NASB).

These immortal words from the pen of Solomon, the wisest man who ever lived, were almost our son Jim's epitaph.

My husband was recovering from bypass surgery in Houston, Texas, and I was by his side when we received an emergency phone call from our home in Colorado. A doctor was on the other end of the line. Our thirteen-year-old son, Jim, was in the hospital with a broken back and arm, but "he was doing just fine." Isn't it amazing how doctors can mystify a person with their coolness over loved ones even when the loved ones may be near death?

Talk about being between a rock and a hard place—I could not leave my husband in his weakened condition to travel home alone, nor could I go to our son. The burden was too heavy to carry, so I laid it down at the feet of Jesus and trusted Him to care for our son in my absence.

We returned home nearly a week later and stopped by the hospital to visit our son and hear his story firsthand.

He had been riding a motorcycle with some friends out in the open fields over hill and dale and was not as familiar with the area as some of the other boys. Jim was following Brian but not close enough to notice that after Brian came up from a dip in the earth, he turned right. Jim came up from the dip, too, and went straight ahead. In shocked disbelief he saw looming in front of him a yawning chasm at least thirty-feet wide and twenty-feet deep. He let go of the handle bars and flew through the air. He doesn't remember landing or much of anything except pain and numbness in his legs. Jim tried to crawl out of the deep cleft, but the slope was too steep; so his buddies pulled him out, set him on the back of a motorcycle, and drove him home.

Every time I run this story through my mind, I know Jim's angel was with him all the time holding him. If the angel had not been, his well-meaning buddies, pulling and stretching his broken back, and then bouncing him on the motorcycle ride home, would probably have paralyzed him.

Yes, at times there is a way that seems right to us, but the end thereof is disastrous.

Why are Proverbs 3:5-6 (NASB) such important verses of Scripture for us?

> Trust in the Lord with all your heart,
> And do not lean on your own understanding.
> In all your ways acknowledge Him,
> And He will make your paths straight.

God wants to teach us that by walking *with* Him we do not have to fear great chasms and crooked pathways looming in front of us. The psalmist said, "Thy word is a lamp unto my feet, and a light unto my path" (Ps. 119: 105).

32
Free as a Bird

Tweety is an American Roller. No, he is not on the Olympic roller-skating team. Tweety is a tiny male canary whose owner is our Joe.

Day after day he raises his glorious voice in songs of praise to his Creator. He lives in an ordinary bird cage but is allowed to fly free on the average of once a day for half an hour. He has a personality all his own, and sometimes it's very childlike, especially at bedtime. He will begin to sing loudly at 8:00 or 9:00 PM in hope we won't cover his cage, and he won't have to sleep. He has been a source of joy for nearly two years.

I am always amazed at how much he sings in his cage. How can he be happy caged in such a small area? Perhaps he really feels free and that freedom makes him sing. I don't know the answer because I can only relate in human terms. Tweety is free to be the sweet, singing creature God created him to be. As Christians we are free too. We have freedom we don't even recognize. We are free in Christ to be the persons He created us to be. First Peter 2:16 says:

> Act as free men, and do not use your freedom as a covering for evil, but use it as bondslaves of God. "If you abide in My word, then you are truly disciples of Mine; and you

shall know the truth, and the truth shall make you free (John 8:31-32, NASB).

Because of our God-given freedom in Christ, the apostle Paul gives us a command in Galatians 5:1: "Stand fast therefore in the liberty wherewith Christ hath made us free, and be not entangled again with the yoke of bondage."

We can be incarcerated and yet be free. Paul and Silas found themselves in the predicament. They were in jail with their feet in stocks and yet singing and praising God at midnight. Their spirits were free. When we know who we are in Christ, regardless of the circumstances, we too can sing and praise God. "If therefore the Son shall make you free, you shall be free indeed" (John 8:36, NASB).

33
Jesus, the Master Painter

Opening an old can of Gesso I wondered if it was still pliable and creamy.

After prying off the lid and peering inside, it looked useless. The white liquid had turned solid, but the top of it was slightly tacky to the touch. That little bit of stickiness encouraged me to add some water and try to reconstitute the hardened mess. After adding the water, I stirred and stirred and stirred until my arm felt like dropping. Perseverance and patience usually pay off. It became like a bubbly shaving cream. At last I could use it.

Gesso is a marvelous thick, water-base foundation for artists to cover a multitude of sins and mistakes on their canvases or boards.

I had several old, ugly, half-finished paintings that needed the Gesso treatment so I could paint a new picture on top of the old. Humming to myself, I began slapping white paint all over my painting boards and the floor as well. *Oh, how lovely,* I thought. *It's just like Jesus giving us a new canvas to paint on each and every day.*

Slowly the unfinished painting began to disappear. It took three or four coats to cover the past completely.

Looking at those old paintings only brought on sadness. But now I was looking at a new, white board with expectancy, and my heart just soared. A new opportunity to create something fresh, beautiful, and exciting. Yes, it is true; I can see the impression of the former painting, but the board is white again. I am free to paint anything on it I wish.

Isn't that just like our lives? We take our paint pots and brushes and go to work trying to create an illusion, trying to create our own life-styles our own ways. One day we stand back to admire our work and put our painting into perspective only to discover it's really out of focus, very old and very ugly. What we do next is the most crucial part in a painting.

We can keep on painting on the horrid-looking painting and hope it will get better with time. That rarely, if ever, happens. We might decide it's so awful that it isn't worth working on anymore, so we throw it in the trash. That is visual deception and never true.

We can ask Jesus to come scrape off the past and paint white over the whole mess so we can start afresh. That's called confession, repentance, and restoration. Jesus willingly gives us our choice of how we would like our painting to proceed.

David knew how this problem felt and expressed it in Psalm 51. He confessed his sin and repented, and God restored the right spirit within him.

Create in me a clean heart, O God,
And renew a right spirit within me.
Do not cast me away from Thy presence,
And do not take Thy Holy Spirit from me.
Restore to me the joy of Thy salvation,
And sustain me with a willing spirit (Ps. 51:10-12, NASB).

David didn't want to throw his painting away. Neither did he wish to keep painting on the old, sinful one. He did want God to scrape off the past and repaint it white so he could live with a clear, clean conscience and have the right to start over. He was willing to turn the paints and brushes over to the Master Artist and let Him continue the painting that he had interrupted.

The Brush

Life started out like a canvas
    And God started painting on me.
But I took the paint brush from Jesus
    And I painted what I wished to see.

The colors I chose kept running;
    The objects were all out of size.
I had made a mess of my painting
    My way now seemed so unwise.

So I brought my painting to Jesus
    The colors - the objects all wrong.
In the markets of earth it was worthless,
    But His brush made my painting belong.

He worked with no condemnation;
    Never mentioned the mess I had made.
He dipped His brush in the rainbow
    And signed it, "The price has been paid."

When I gave the brush back to Jesus,
    When I gave the brush back to Him,
He started all over, my life's canvas to fill
    When I gave to Jesus the brush of my will.
                     —Author Unknown

34
Near-death on Ararat

In the late summer of 1982, my husband took a group of eleven men with him to Eastern Turkey to climb Mount Ararat. Their objective was to relocate the biblical ark of Noah. There had been many reports of seeing a long dark object at the 15,000-foot level. They hoped it was the old boat. All were anxious to find the ark and looked day after day, but to no avail. The last day Jim decided to leave the group that was high on the mountain and return to base camp.

One rule of the group was, "Never hike alone." Jim broke his own rule. He headed back toward base camp to begin the process of breaking camp. He never arrived.

Somewhere along the way he was hit by a rock slide. He remembers a snowfield he needed to cross, so he sat down to put on his crampons. (Crampons are much like an old-fashioned roller skate that clamps on the bottom of your hiking boot. They are metalic and have many sharp teeth on the bottom for walking on the ice.) He awakened many hours later to find himself among the rocks and covered with blood. Evening was fast approaching, and he knew he had to get his sleeping bag out of his backpack. The temperatures can be extreme on Mount Ararat. Without warning sudden electrical or snow storms appear.

Jim was able to crawl to the shelter of a huge rock and place his sleeping bag there. A moment later he was snuggled in for the night and ready for sleep.

Suddenly a large boulder broke loose from upslope and headed right for him. It hit the sheltering rock, bounced, and skimmed over his prone form. All he could think of before he lapsed into unconsciousness once again was: "The Lord is my rock, and my fortress, and my deliverer" (2 Sam. 22:2, KJV).

Through much prayer, Jim's men found him the next morning, nursed his wounds, and put him on a horse headed for base camp. From camp it was a four-hour horseback ride down the mountain. Another three or four hours passed before he arrived at a military hospital.

After the plastic surgeon sewed up all of Jim's head and facial wounds, someone placed a phone call to me for him. He assured me that he was quite all right and that I did not need come to him. (That was before he looked in a mirror.)

The graciousness of Almighty God never ceases to amaze me. Jim never felt any pain throughout his ordeal except when jostled by the horseback ride down the mountain. He does admit to pain when the surgeon stitched him without the benefit of any anesthetic.

One week later he hobbled through our front door on feet and ankles that were so swollen he could barely walk. My mind could not comprehend what my eyes saw. I burst into tears. He was the most pitiful sight I had ever seen. In spite of four or five missing front teeth, the smile on his face was about the only positive thing I saw. I knew we were in for a long recovery.

Once again, the grace of God came through. Exactly one month from the accident, Jim was flying toward Eastern Turkey once again. This time I was at his side. We needed to check out one more sighting.

Looking back over the whole incident, I am fully persuaded of one outstanding truth. The only safe place to be is in Jesus our Rock. Thank you Jesus for being that Rock.

35
The Severed Branch

"Mom, Jill's dead." Those terrifying words pierced through to my conscious level as I napped. Sitting straight up in my bed, I could feel the color drain from my face as the adrenaline pumped hard. "What happened?" I asked as I buttoned my robe. "She fell out of the tree and isn't moving," was her reply.

I ran to the side of my eight-year-old child where she lay on the ground from her fall. She was gasping for air as I knelt beside her. "Am I going to die, Mom?" Her question was barely audible as her brown eyes searched my face for an answer. My heart was aching to reassure her with a no, but I really didn't know. Falling from nearly two stories had temporarily knocked the wind out of her.

All kinds of thoughts gallop crazily through a parent's mind in a moment like this, and Jill's penetrating question hadn't helped the situation.

I began to check her over very carefully to determine if she had a severe injury. She didn't seem to, so I carried her tenderly to her bed, treated her for shock, and called an ambulance.

While we waited for the ambulance, I began questioning her. The disaster occurred when she had stepped from a strong, thick limb to a small, rotten one; and it broke, dashing her to the ground in terror. When the branch became severed from the tree, it caused separation and devastation.

Jesus said, "If anyone separates from me, he is thrown away like a useless branch, withers, and is gathered into a pile with all the others and burned" (John 15:6, TLB). That's not a very pretty picture, I admit. That is why it is essential to stay attached to the Vine.

Jesus said that He was the Vine and we are the branches and that we must abide in Him and He will abide (to remain, to dwell) with us.

Take care to live in Me, and let Me live in you. For a branch can't produce fruit when severed from the vine. Nor can you be fruitful apart from Me. Yes, I am the Vine; you are the branches. Whoever lives in Me and I in him shall produce a large crop of fruit. For apart from Me, you can't do a thing (John 15:4-5, TLB).

Let us take care, beloved, not to become separated from the Vine but constantly abide in Him. We can do all things through Christ who gives us strength.

36
Fortification Against Coyotes

Big Red was a marvelous overweight red rooster. On the other end of the scale was Henry, a frightened whimp of a chicken. If you looked at him wrong, he would squeak and run the other way. Because of Big Red's size, he could not run like the other roosters; his gait was a cross between a waddle and a hippity-hop. He had so much character the children would chase him just to watch him run.

We had borrowed four roosters of different varieties and different sizes to pull sentry duty in my garden. They did a wonderful job on the grasshoppers. I had promised to return them to their owners at the end of the garden season. All summer the four would trail after me softly clucking while I weeded each garden row. When I wasn't in the garden, they would crow up a storm. One would start, usually Big Red, and the others soon followed suit. They would crow day and night!

Our son Jim would wait until the chickens went to roost for the night then sneak out to their house and crow a couple of times. Sure enough, the roosters would get cranked up and answer him. Each one was unique and had a certain crow; we could always tell which one was crowing.

One morning I went out to take them a little grain. *How strange,* I thought, *they are not at the corner of the fence to meet me.* I began calling. No chickens! Stepping over the fence I saw what I wished I hadn't: a trail of feathers. I felt so sad inside as I followed the trail to the other end of the garden and over the fence. Just over the fence in the tall grass were a few remains. I knew they had been carried away and eaten by the coyotes that roam our fields. My emotions hit bottom. The roosters had been my borrowed, faithful friends; now they were gone.

The Bible says, "Be of sober spirit, be on alert. Your adversary, the devil, prowls about like a roaring lion, seeking someone to devour" (1 Pet. 5:8, NASB). The coyotes must have been pretty sneaky, fast, and quiet because we never heard any noise from the chickens.

Satan is as fast and sneaky as a coyote and always looking for an unsuspecting victim. For this reason James tells us to: "Submit yourselves therefore to God. Resist the devil, and he will flee from you" (4:7).

Be on alert, brethren, put up a spiritual fight, and take a stand against the enemy. The result of this type of warfare is: the devil has to leave. Praise God, there is victory against the enemy of our souls as we put ourselves under the command of King Jesus.

Finally, be strong in the Lord, and in the strength of His might. Put on the *full armor* of God, that you may be able to stand firm against the schemes of the devil. For our struggle is not against flesh and blood, but against the rulers, against the powers, against the world forces of this darkness, against the spiritual forces of wickedness in the heavenly places. Therefore, take up the full armor of God, that you may be able to resist in the evil day, and having done everything, to stand firm. Stand firm, therefore, having *girded your loins with truth,* and having put on the *breastplate of righteousness,* and having *shod your feet* with the preparation of *the gospel of peace;* in addition to all, taking up the *shield of faith* with which you will be able to extinguish all the flaming missiles of the evil one. And take the *helmet of salvation,* and the *sword* of the Spirit, which *is the word of God*" (Eph. 6:10-17, NASB; author's italics).

When we put on our spiritual armor, we never, never, never take it off. We don't put it on each morning; we never take it off after it's first donned. We go to bed with it on. We may tell Jesus, as we go to bed at night, each piece of armor we have on and what it's purpose is. The enemy will hear us, too, and know that we are ready for battle. We will not be caught unaware.

The chickens were caught unaware at night while the enemy prowled around seeking what it could devour. We need stay alert, always ready for battle. When we resist the devil, he will flee from us.